Copyright © 2006 by Chronicle Books LLC.
All rights reserved.

Book design by Sara Gillingham.
Text by Traci N. Todd.
Typeset in Volta and Toronto Subway.
Manufactured in China.

Library of Congress Cataloging-in-Publication Data
A is for astronaut : exploring space from A to Z.
p. cm.
ISBN-13: 978-0-8118-5462-7
ISBN-10: 0-8118-5462-0
1. Outer space—Exploration—Juvenile literature.
2. Vocabulary—Juvenile literature.
QB500.262.A3 2006
919.904—dc22
2005026852

Distributed in Canada by Raincoast Books
9050 Shaughnessy Street, Vancouver, British Columbia V6P 6E5

10 9 8 7 6 5 4 3 2

Chronicle Books LLC
680 Second Street, San Francisco, California 94107

www.chroniclekids.com

A Is for Astronaut

Exploring Space from A to Z

chronicle books · san francisco

Asteroid
a space rock that's smaller than a planet and orbits the Sun

Astronaut
a person who explores space

Apollo 11
the first mission to land a person on the Moon

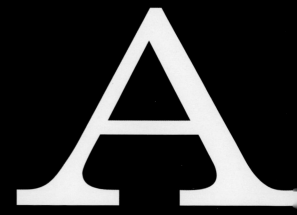

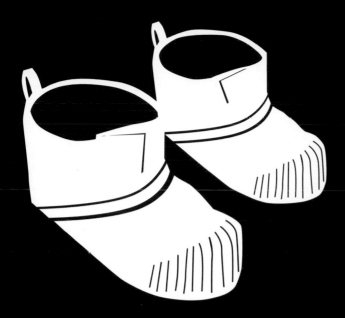

Boots
an important part of an
astronaut's space suit

B

Booster
a rocket that pushes
spacecraft into the air

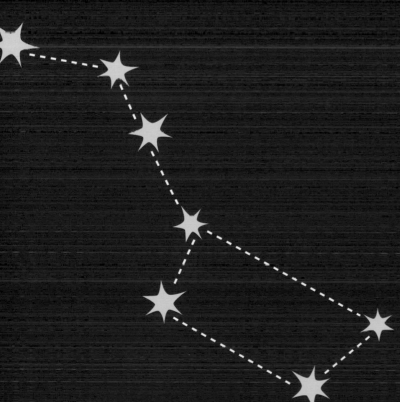

Big Dipper
a group of stars that looks like a big spoon

C

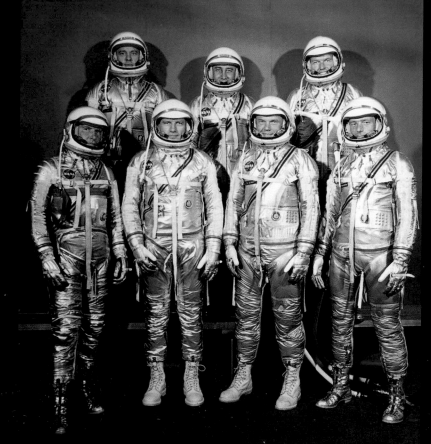

Cockpit
the part of a spacecraft where the pilot sits

Crew
the people who help the pilot fly a spacecraft

Comet
a ball of ice with a tail made of dust and gas

Dinner

cookies, cheese spread, creamed spinach, candy, crackers, and beef steak—yum!

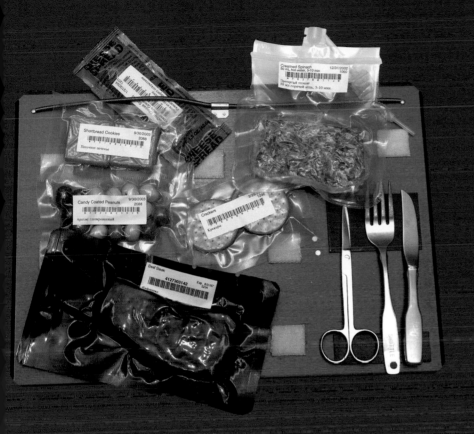

"Dirty Snowball"

another name for a comet

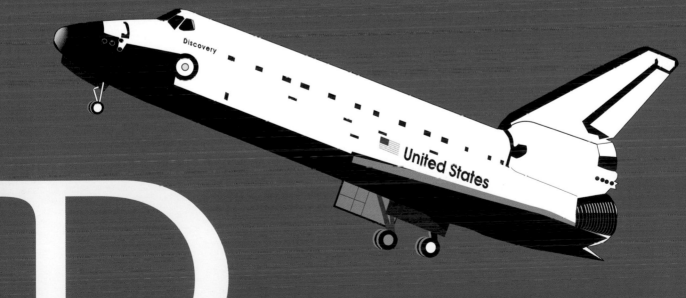

D

Discovery

a space shuttle first launched in 1984

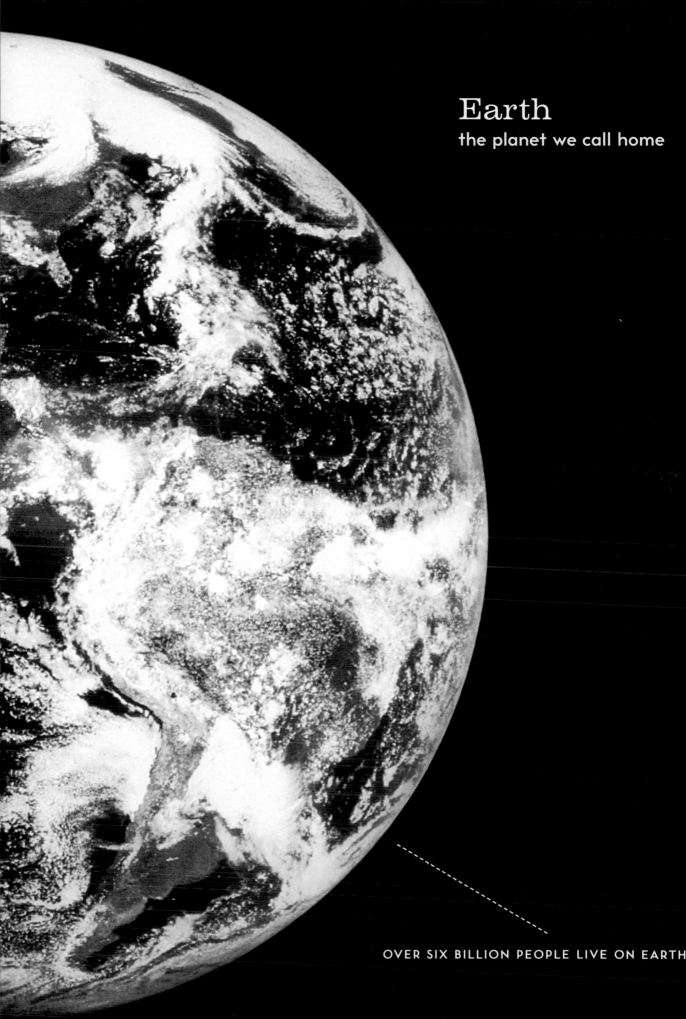

Earth
the planet we call home

OVER SIX BILLION PEOPLE LIVE ON EARTH

F

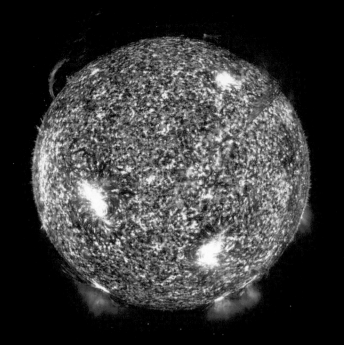

Flares
bursts of energy that flash from the Sun

Falling Stars
bits of rock and debris that
fall to Earth from space

Footprint
left on the Moon by
astronaut Buzz Aldrin

Galaxy

a large group of stars and planets

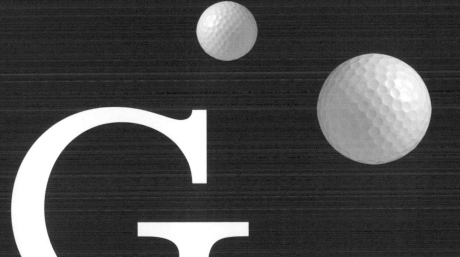

G

Golf Balls

left on the Moon by
astronaut Alan Shepard

Hubble Space Telescope
a telescope that floats high above
Earth taking pictures of space

Halley's Comet
appears every 75 to 76 years

Ham
the first chimpanzee
in space

H

UNLATCH COVER
WHEN NOT IN USE

I

International Space Station
a structure in space where astronauts can live

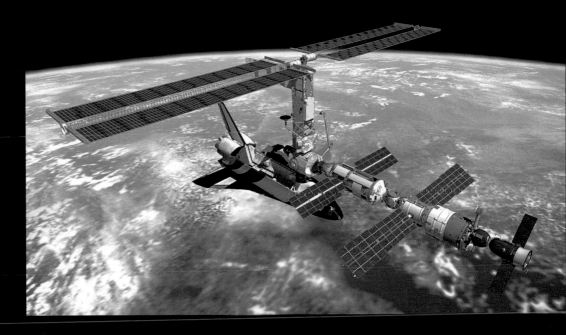

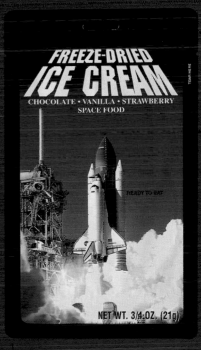

Ice Cream
freeze-dried, an astronaut's treat

Ignition
the starting of the engines that launch a spacecraft

J

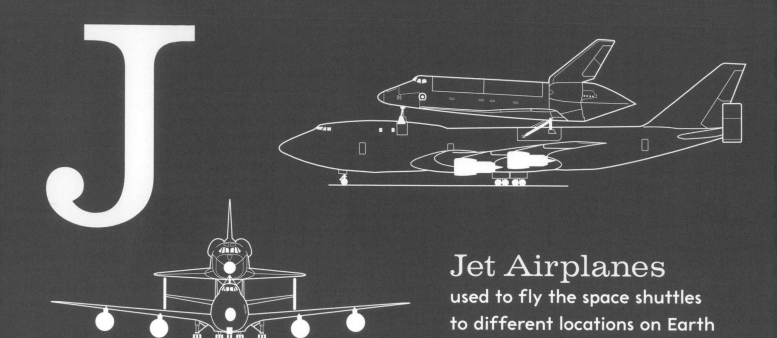

Jet Airplanes
used to fly the space shuttles
to different locations on Earth

John Glenn
who, in 1962, was the
first U.S. astronaut to
pilot a spacecraft
around the Earth

Kennedy Space Center
in Florida, where the space shuttles are launched

K

Launchpad
where spacecraft lift off

5,

4,

3,

2,

1

Liftoff!

L

Laika
one of the first dogs
to journey into space

Mission Control
where scientists control the NASA space missions

M

THE MOON ORBITING EARTH

Moon
orbits Earth and is most easily seen at night

N

NASA
the National Aeronautics and
Space Administration, in charge
of the American space program

Neil Armstrong
the first man to walk on the Moon

Netherlands

Norway
two countries helping to build
the International Space Station

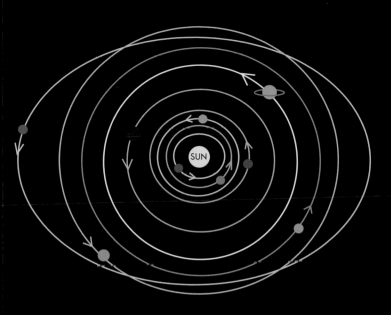

Orbit
the path planets take around the Sun
and moons take around the planets

Oxygen Pack
a tank that stores the oxygen
astronauts need to breathe
in space

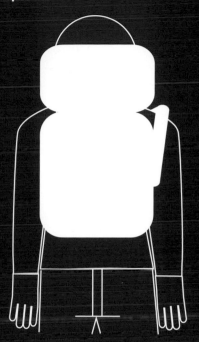

Observatory
a building from which you can
see planets, moons, and stars

Planets
there are nine known
in our solar system

JUPITER

MARS

VENUS

EARTH

MERCURY

SUN

URANUS

PLUTO

NEPTUNE

SATURN

P

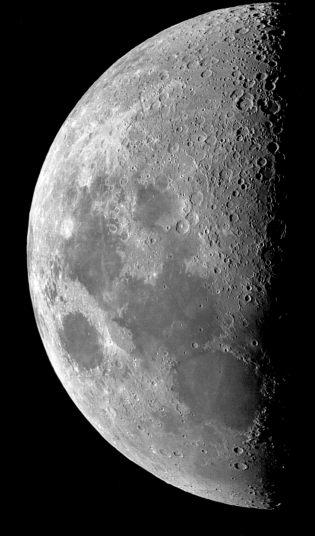

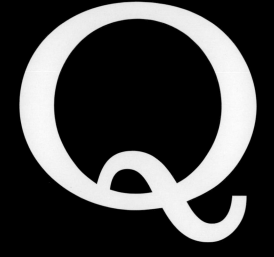

Quarter Moon
when the Moon looks half full in the sky

THE PHASES OF THE MOON

NEW MOON   CRESCENT   QUARTER   GIBBOUS   FULL MOON   GIBBOUS   QUARTER   CRESCENT   NEW MOON

Quasar
a red object in space
that resembles a star

Rover
a vehicle, like a car, used to explore the Moon and planets

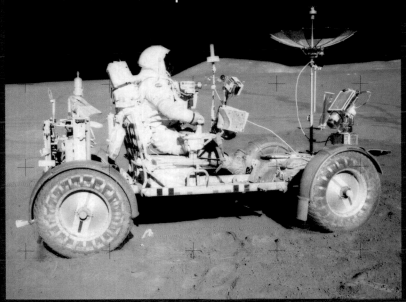

Robotic Arm
a machine that helps astronauts perform dangerous tasks

R

Radar
a system used to find faraway objects

Space Suit
the suit astronauts wear
to keep them safe in space

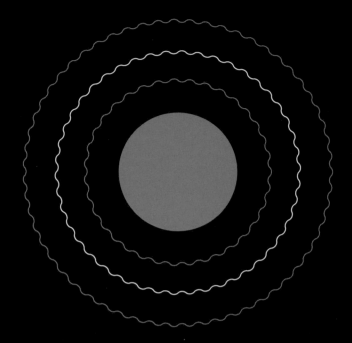

Sun
the large star that gives
Earth heat and light

Satellite
anything natural or human-made
that orbits a larger object in space

Telescope
an instrument you can use
to see the planets and stars

T

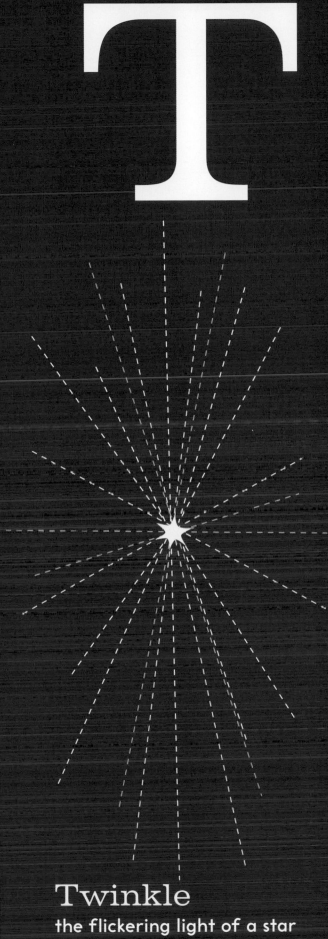

Twinkle
the flickering light of a star

Universe

every planet, moon, and star in our galaxy and beyond

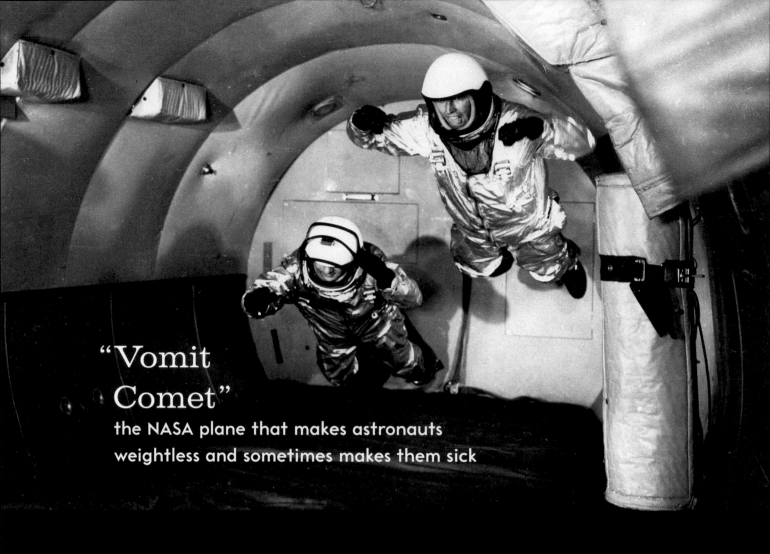

"Vomit Comet"
the NASA plane that makes astronauts
weightless and sometimes makes them sick

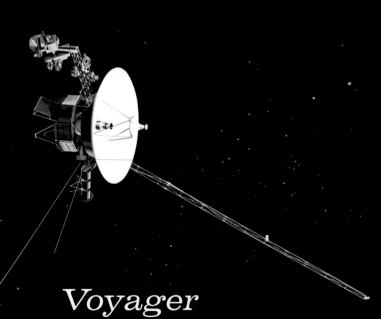

Voyager
spacecraft that explore space farther
than any human-made machine has
ever explored . . . so far

V

W

World
Space
Week

celebrated every year from
October 4 to October 10

Weightlessness
the reason things float in space

Wright Brothers
the first people to successfully fly an airplane

XS-1 Rocket Plane
the first plane to fly faster than the speed of sound

Planet X
the name scientists give a planet they think exists but haven't found yet

X-15 Rocket Plane
a super-fast plane that helped scientists in the 1960s understand space flight

Yuri Gagarin
in 1961 became the first human space traveler

SEASONS IN
THE NORTHERN
HEMISPHERE

FALL

SUMMER

WINTER

SPRING

Y

Year
the length of time it takes
Earth to orbit around the Sun

Zoom! Z

Image Credits